Cloud Computing:
A Guide for Executives
& Business Owners

Charles Henson

Nashville Computer

277 Wilson Pike Cr #100

Brentwood, TN 37027

615-377-0054

www.NashvilleComputer.com

Helping Small to Medium Sized Business Owners
Eliminate Technology Headaches Finally and Forever

Printed in the USA.

Contents

Introduction

I am sure you have heard of Cloud Computing whether it was in a meeting, or you saw the commercials from Microsoft, Cisco and other mega companies trying to get the word "Cloud" into your brain. The problem with all this media hype is, it doesn't tell you or explain what the "Cloud" really encompasses.

This is why I wanted to set the record straight and provide business owners and executives a simple, easy to read book that would explain what Cloud Computing is, how it can help your business, how it can possibly save you money and what you need to know in order to make the best decisions when choosing a Cloud vendor.

Cloud Computing is NOT a good fit for every company; and if you don't get all the facts or fully understand the pros and cons, you can end up making some VERY costly decisions that can drastically affect your business.

That said, for most clients, Cloud Computing can eliminate IT capital expenditures and actually lower your overall IT costs by 10% to 40%. This greatly improves the ability for remote workers to connect and work, simplifies their entire IT infrastructure and solves numerous technology problems that were being worked around for years.

My hope is by the end of this book you'll have a much better understanding of Cloud Computing. Of course, my company is always available as a resource for a second opinion or quick question, so please feel free to contact my office direct if we can clarify any points made in this book or answer any questions you have.

Dedicated to serving you,

Charles Henson

Chapter 1

A Technology Journey

Remember the days of the VHS camera that was so big it had to sit on your shoulder, the GPS that didn't know about new roads or where construction existed, the pager you wore on your belt to get a message or number displayed to call? Do you remember the "Brick" cell phone that was heavy and dropped calls consistently? Do you remember the desktop that took 2 minutes to boot, the early days of the Internet when it took even longer to download a picture? Well as time changes, so does the technology. Each of these items have been replaced or enhanced over time. Today, the Smartphone has ALL of the above capabilities in a small pocket sized device. These units can browse the web, search for the nearest local restaurant or gas station; they can navigate you through the streets of New York City, LA, Chicago and most everywhere else whether driving or walking. Applications (apps) installed on these devices can scan a barcode and tell you who has the best price on the item scanned or the full details of its contents. My favorite is the WordPress app which allows you to signup, build, and customize a website and blog from your phone.

How about the movie industry? Remember driving out to Blockbuster video and renting the latest movie on VHS, having to remember to take it back within five days to avoid a daily late fee? Then, they started renting DVD's that could get scratched and the movie would have skips. Then Netflix offered to send you a DVD to your mailbox so you didn't have to drive anywhere to pick it up. You could keep the movie as long as you like and had a flat monthly fee. Then, Redbox came along and offered the .99 cents per night rental option. Netflix fought back by having the ability to stream the movie across the Internet. Today, you can watch any movie any time and from anywhere as long as you have an Internet connection. This is also available on Smartphones, iPads, Kindles and other handheld devices.

And then there's the music industry... Music came on vinyl discs and would be played on a turntable with the needle reading the disc, then 8 tracks, cassettes and then compact disk (CD). Music stores used to be plentiful and a fun place to hang out. You could listen to certain parts of a CD or its songs and buy the album after sampling it. But after the birth of the MP3 and Apple introducing a way to buy single songs for only .99 cents, download them, and listen on-the-go or create your own custom CD's, the music stores dried up. As of June 2011 Apple has introduced its iCloud and Google has released their version of Cloud Music. These services allow you to upload your music to a remote server on the Internet and listen to your music anytime anywhere.

Computers are another technology that has drastically changed. Starting out as a single unit taking up an entire room and only able to do a simple math problem, to the tablet PC's of today that fit in the palm of your hand, technology advancements have been huge.

As you can see by just these few examples, technology continues to change and each generation seems to have a better more efficient way of doing things. With this, the price keeps dropping and the abilities seem to grow. So is your business ready for its IT infrastructure (computer network) to drastically change?

Chapter 2

What Is Cloud Computing?

There is no true definition of "Cloud Computing". I believe the best definition is: A general term for anything that involves delivering hosted services or applications on a remote server accessed across the Internet.

Imagine your current desktop or laptop environment at work with all of its applications, icons, desktop wallpaper, personal photos, shortcuts, favorites and settings being the same no matter which device you connect from. You will have the same desktop environment whether you log in from work, from your iPad, a library PC, friends or coworker's laptop or a hotel PC. Additionally you will have access to the same files and folders from each. If you leave your e-mail and or Excel spreadsheet open while working at home, you can continue working right where you left off once you have arrived at your office. It is also the same if traveling and check into your hotel, once connected to the Internet. If you lose your laptop or it dies, you can just grab another device and continue where you left off. All of your applications and files are stored in the "Cloud".

Another easy way to not only understand Cloud Computing but also gain insight into why it's gaining in popularity is to compare it to the evolution of public utilities. For example, let's look at the evolution of electricity.

Back in the industrial age, factories had to produce their own power in order to run the machines that produced the hard goods they manufactured. Be it textiles or railroad spikes, using machines gave these companies enormous competitive advantages by producing more goods with fewer workers and in less time. For many years the production of power was every bit as important to their company's success as the skill of their workers and quality of their products.

This put factories into TWO businesses: the business of producing their goods and the business of producing power. Then the concept of delivering power (electricity) as a utility was introduced by Thomas Edison when he developed a commercial grade replacement for gas lighting and heating using centrally generated and distributed electricity. From there, as they say, the rest was history.

The concept of electric current being generated in central power plants and delivered to factories as a utility caught on fast. This meant manufacturers no longer had to be in the business of producing their own power. **In fact, in a very short period of time, it became a competitive necessity for factories to take**

advantage of the lower cost option being offered by public utilities. Almost overnight, thousands of steam engines and electric generators were rendered obsolete and left to rust next to the factories they used to power.

What made this possible was a series of inventions and scientific breakthroughs but what drove the demand was pure economics. Utility companies were able to leverage economies of scale that single manufacturing plants simply couldn't match in output or in price. In fact, the price of power dropped so significantly that it quickly became affordable for not only factories but every single household in the country.

Today, we are in a similar transformation following a similar course. The only difference is that instead of cheap and plentiful electricity, advancements in technology and Internet connectivity are driving down the costs of computing power. With Cloud Computing, businesses can pay for "computing power" like a utility without having the exorbitant costs of installing, hosting and supporting it.

In fact, you are probably already experiencing the benefits of Cloud Computing in some way but hadn't realized it. Below are a number of Cloud Computing applications, also called SaaS or "software as a service," you might be using:

- Gmail, Hotmail or other free e-mail accounts
- Facebook
- NetSuite, Salesforce.com
- Constant Contact, Exact Target, Aweber or other e-mail broadcasting services
- Zoomerang, SurveyMonkey and other survey tools
- LinkedIn
- Twitter
- All things Google (Search, Apps, Calendar share, AdWords, Maps, etc.)
- Flickr.com, Photobucket.com (picture storing and sharing)

If you think about it, almost every single application you use today can be (or already is) being put "in the Cloud" where you can access it and pay for it via your Internet browser for a monthly fee or utility based pricing. You don't purchase and install software but instead access it via an Internet browser or remote application and pay only for what you use.

What About Office 365 And Google Apps?

Office 365 and Google Apps are perfect examples of the Cloud Computing trend; for an inexpensive monthly fee, you can get full access and use of Office applications that used to cost a few hundred dollars to purchase. And, since these apps are being powered by the Cloud provider, you don't need an expensive desktop with lots of resources to use them – just a simple Internet connection will do on a laptop, desktop or tablet or even a Smartphone.

These applications may not be a good fit for your business and each application needs to be looked at closely. Neither Google Apps nor Office365 (currently) integrate with many line-of-business applications, which presents a deal breaker for using this service. For example, if you like using Microsoft's Excel or Word to pull reports or create documents from your line of business application, you might not be able to do that with these services. If you want to export or import information from one program to another such as exporting financial information directly from QuickBooks or other accounting software to an Excel spreadsheet, then these online versions will not work effectively.

Microsoft's Office 365 is too early in its first release to risk moving your critical company operations to. At this point not to mention a number of other limitations that would make it a poor choice for a business, including the fact that you get zero help desk support. If something goes wrong, there isn't a customer service help desk you can call for support or assistance. But again, these types of hosted applications are perfect examples of where we are going with

Cloud Computing. Please note that you cannot get help with these applications from the vendors directly but can from your Cloud Integrator or IT admin.

Microsoft's founder, Bill Gates vision was to have a computer on every desk and in every home. As of this writing Microsoft is BETA testing a hosted desktop experience (VDI: Virtual Desktop Infrastructure) so before long you will no longer need a local desktop or PC. As mentioned earlier, technology continues to evolve and change.

Chapter 3

Pros and Cons of Moving To the Cloud

As you read this section, keep in mind there is no "perfect" solution. All options, be it an in-house network or a Cloud based solution have both advantages and disadvantages. Cloud based solutions have to be determined on a case-by-case basis and needs thorough consideration before you can come to a complete conclusion on which option will work for you. (Warning: Do not let a non-Cloud expert tell you there is only "one way" of doing something.) Most companies end up with a **hybrid solution** where some of their applications are in the Cloud and some are still hosted and maintained from an in-house server. We'll discuss more of this in a later chapter; however, here are the general pros and cons of Cloud Computing:

Pros of Cloud Computing:

- Lowered IT costs.

This is probably the single most compelling reason why companies choose to move their network (all or in part) to the Cloud. Not only do you save money on software licenses, but hardware (servers and workstations) as well as in IT support and upgrades. In fact, we save our clients an average of 10% to 40% when we move some or part of their network functionality to the Cloud. So if you hate constantly writing big, fat checks for IT upgrades, you'll really want to look into Cloud Computing. Included in this book I will discuss how we've done this for other clients and what the savings have been.

- The ability to access your desktop and/or applications from anywhere using any device.

If you travel a lot, have remote workers or prefer to use an iPad while traveling and a laptop at your house, Cloud Computing will give you the ability to work from any of these devices. Whether you get snowed in or have an employee with a sick child at home, the ability to work remotely can be huge. Have a court docket but the power is out? Grab your laptop and run to the nearest coffee shop or restaurant, jump on their Internet and grab your documents. Have a four hour flight? Most airlines today offer Wi-Fi for a fee and it will allow you to access your Cloud desktop while literally being in the clouds.

- Disaster recovery & business continuity.

The server in your office may be extremely vulnerable to a number of threats including viruses, human error, hardware failure, software corruption and, of course, physical damage due to a fire, flood or other natural disasters. If your server was in the Cloud and (God forbid) your office was reduced to a pile of rubble, you could purchase a new laptop and be back up and running within the same day. (Your data is not where you are when you're using Cloud Computing). This would NOT be the case if you had a traditional network and were using tape drives, CDs, USB drives or other physical storage devices to back up your system.

Plus, like a public utility, Cloud platforms are far more robust and secure than your average business network because they can utilize economies of scale to invest heavily into security, redundancy and failover systems making them far less likely to go down. Data Centers (aka collocations) are setup with multiple points of failure. The data center your Cloud environment is hosted in should have redundant Internet providers, redundant air conditioning, redundant battery backups and backup generators that have full contracts to keep them running for days.

- It's faster, cheaper and easier to set up new employees.

If you have a seasonal workforce or a lot of turnover, Cloud Computing will not only lower your costs of setting up new accounts, but it will make it infinitely faster.

- You use it without having to "own" it.

More specifically, you don't own the *responsibility and risk* of having to install, update and maintain the infrastructure. Think of it similar to living in a condo where someone else takes care of the building maintenance, repairing the roof and mowing the lawn, but you still have the only key to your section of the building and use of all the facilities. This is particularly attractive for companies who are new or expanding, but don't want the heavy outlay of capital for purchasing and supporting an expensive computer network.

- It's a "greener" technology that will save on power and your electric bill.

For some smaller companies, the power savings will be too small to measure. However, for larger companies with multiple servers who are cooling a hot server room and keep their servers running 24/7/365, the savings are considerable.

- Scalable.

The Cloud technology model allows you to grow your business and its IT usage on an as needed basis. I will cover this in more detail in Chapter 11.

Cons of Cloud Computing:

- An Internet or power outage.

While you can mitigate this risk by using a commercial grade Internet connection and maintaining a second backup connection, there is always a chance that you'll lose Internet connectivity. If the power in your office goes down, the secondary Internet connection is a mute point. Either loosing just Internet or total power, these will make it impossible to work from your local devices in your place of business. I will discuss this and offer more information and how to address this under the "What to Look for When Hiring a Cloud Integrator" later on in this book. However I want you to try and remember the last time your building power went out or your Internet connection at work failed. Also don't forget that you can use your laptop and a wireless Internet connection from your Smartphone while the power is off.

- Data types and file size.

Many companies use basic Office applications, a CRM, and an accounting program. However, more and more companies are moving to paperless and or are working with much larger files than in the past. AutoCAD is a program for draying and designing items from bridges to house, to general landscape. These rendered drawings can scale to very large files.

Additionally, Doctors are working with very high quality x-ray images. Working with either of these file types require a high end graphics card and a lot of system resources. These large file types are handled in a hybrid Cloud solution. You'll find more information on this in chapter 5.

- Non compatible line-of-business applications.

Line of business applications would be the primary program that your business cannot live without. An example would be a contractor that uses a program to do all bidding and job estimates. This one particular company would love to integrate their software into a Cloud environment due to the amount of remote sales and construction people needing access to the data. The issue came about with the software program that was mandated to be used by the insurance companies they do work for. This application would allow multiple people to work simultaneously in the Cloud but if one user closed out, it would corrupt everyone else's projects. The company is forced to run this application in a traditional network environment. This particular software company is currently working on an updated version of this as Cloud Computing is becoming more popular and the insurance industry and contractors are pushing the software maker to get this issue resolved. Each application needs to be tested and verified it will work in a Cloud environment before taking the leap.

- Working Offline.

There are times you will want to work on files or programs while you are not connected to the Internet. This is a concern to some users and is being addressed through replication of data between devices. File synchronization is being tested and Citrix now has a program function that will allow you to checkout files and return them once re-connected. You can copy files from your Cloud solution to your local device but it is currently a manual process. This is another place that a hybrid Cloud can allow you to sync files to your local server from your PC and replicate to the Cloud.

Chapter 4

Cloud Versus a Traditional Network:
A Comparison of Costs

As stated earlier, each client has a slightly unique set of circumstances and needs that will factor into the cost savings and benefits. But in order to know what the savings are we recommend that you compare the Cloud cost over a 3-4 year period since that is the normal span of time when most all workstations and servers need to be replaced and software upgraded. This will help account for the fact that you don't have to purchase new hardware as often (which is a huge cost savings when moving to the Cloud).

The cost savings are often compelling enough for business owners to take the dive into Cloud Computing; and if carefully planned, that dive can help eliminate downtime and security risks are greatly minimized. You cannot truly compare a Cloud solution to what you have paid in the past for IT. You need to look at it from the standpoint of, if I replaced my entire IT infrastructure and maintained it as a business should, how do they compare? The true cost of ownership (TKO) has to be factored in. By using a Cloud solution you can budget monthly for not just the hosting of your desktops and applications but also you can gain access to a help desk for your users to rely on. When getting a Cloud quote you should also get a quote on overhauling your current IT infrastructure. If you have an employee that is dedicated to the IT department, the TKO increases as that person will no longer need to be on staff.

A Cloud solution is like using the fastest technology and the best of the best computers all the time without having to have an IT person or people to maintain them. In fact, on average clients that comparea traditional versus Cloud solution experience LESS downtime, viruses, spyware, root kits, problems and system crashes than they did with their in-house network.

Chapter 5

Types of Cloud Solutions:

Pure Cloud: This is where all your applications and data are put off premise (in a collocation data center) and are delivered across the Internet and accessed through various devices thin clients, laptops, desktops, iPads, phones and other devices.

Hybrid Cloud: Although "pure" Cloud Computing has valid applications, for many, it's not always possible. A hybrid Cloud enables you to put certain pieces of existing IT infrastructure (say, storage, Office, Documents and e-mail) in the Cloud, and the remainder of the IT infrastructure stays on premise. This gives you the ability to enjoy the costs savings and benefits of Cloud Computing where it makes the most sense without risking your entire environment. An example of this would be an Engineering firm that uses AutoCAD to do huge drawings and renderings which require a very high performance PC and which creates large files. In this environment, you would need a server onsite with the high powered PC's on which to store the large drawing files on and all other business applications would be in the Cloud. The files can be replicated to an offsite for business continuity.

Point Solutions: Another option would be simply to put certain applications, like SharePoint or Microsoft Exchange, in the Cloud while keeping everything else onsite. Since e-mail is usually a critical application that everyone needs and wants access to on the road and on various devices (laptop, tablet, iPad, smart phone, etc.) often this is a great way to get advanced features of Microsoft Exchange without the cost of installing and supporting your own in-house Exchange server. This is also a viable solution when using QuickBooks via the Internet or a CRM such as Salesforce.

Public Cloud: A public Cloud is a service that anyone can tap into with a network connection and a credit card. They are shared infrastructures that allow you to pay-as-you-go and managed through a self-service web portal. An example of this would be Google Apps and Amazon web services. With Amazon, you can "spin" up a server by following through a wizard, answering questions and entering your billing information. Once the server is running you can install applications and work from that remote server unit. Some of the issues are: Where is it? How do I get support? How much does it cost? (Amazon pricing is so complicated that they offer classes on how to price their Cloud model.)

Private Cloud: Private Clouds are essentially self-built infrastructures that mimic public Cloud services, but are on premise. Private Clouds are often the choice of companies who want the benefits of Cloud Computing, but don't want their data held in a public environment. In choosing a private Cloud, you would be responsible for the Internet connectivity, battery backups, data backups, server room infrastructure and the extra power consumption and risk of owning your own IT.

Chapter 6

Internet Connectivity:

The Internet today is such an important tool for businesses. With Cloud Computing all information is transferred securely using the Internet connections coming into your office or from where ever you are accessing the Internet. So the big question I hear a lot is, "what if my Internet connection goes down for an extended period of time"?

Before I give you my answer, I'll ask you a question: When was the last time your Internet went down? While this is a valid concern, Internet connectivity has improved tremendously over the years. Currently we overcome it in the following ways for our clients using the Cloud. We resolve this by requiring a secondary Internet connection, by a second carrier in your area. If you are currently using a T1 provided by AT&T, WindStream, XO Communications or whomever, we would require you to get a secondary Internet connection as a backup. As of this writing, we have a secondary Internet connection via Comcast Business. It is a 12MBps connection and costs less than a $100 per month. Additionally we recommend a firewall appliance that allows seamless failover in the event that one provider's connection fails. With today's ever changing devices, Internet is readily available on your Smartphones or from a coffee shop or restaurant. In a worst case scenario, you can have users go home and access your Cloud desktops from their own home Internet connections. Additionally, you could have users with laptops or handhelds access Wi-Fi from a local coffee shop or restaurant. Today's Smartphone's, iPad's and laptop's have built in wireless so you can access the Internet from almost anywhere. Phone providers are selling their wireless hotspots and most Smartphone's have this ability as well. With this, you can access and work from your Cloud desktop not only if your Internet is down but even if the electric power is off in your business.

Chapter 7

Security:

Security is a huge concern to all people and businesses which leads to a common question I hear frequently. "Isn't there a big risk of someone accessing my data if it's in the Cloud?" In many cases, Cloud Computing is a MORE secure way of accessing and storing data. Just because your server is onsite at your location doesn't make it more secure than being in a remote location; in fact, most small to medium businesses can't justify the cost of securing their network the way a Cloud provider can. And most security breaches occur due to human error; one of your employees downloads a file that contains a virus, they don't use secure passwords, or they simply e-mail confidential information out to people who shouldn't see it. Other security breaches occur in on-site networks because the company didn't properly maintain their own in-house network with security updates, software patches, and up-to-date anti-virus software.

We have had to replace numerous servers and workstations over the years due to theft. There are FAR more common ways networks get compromised versus a Cloud provider getting hacked. Cloud Integrators have strict policies and procedures in place to help eliminate most all security concerns. Business owners are typically to busy running their business to be concerned with local PC and server security. Most small to medium business don't have procedures and policies to eliminate or safeguard from uncontrolled Internet surfing. We recommend that companies moving to the Cloud implement an Internet Usage Policy that restricts Internet usage to ONLY business related surfing. We suggest you block social media, porn, online dating, gambling, etc... These policies can be changed and sites allowed but it is not recommended. If your company doesn't have an Internet usage policy or at least monitor where your employees are surfing the web today then you need to address this ASAP and ask yourself, how secure is my current network?

Let me conclude this chapter by posing a few questions to you. Now for the questions: How secure is your company's network environment and data today?

- Do you allow employees to use their workstations, laptops and other devices to browse the Internet without a content filter?
- Do you allow remote users to use their PC's to remote into your servers via VPN?
- Have you had a desktop or laptop get a virus lately? Spyware? Malware? Rootkits?
- How about a key logger that can record your employees every key stroke including their usernames and password to not only your servers but to your business' online bank accounts?

- Laptop users that have their username, password and VPN address taped to the laptop?

I'm not trying to scare you but the office PC your employees use should not be used for personal use and allowed to have open access to the internet by your employees. You purchase and maintain the infrastructure for running and growing your business, not costing it downtime and more expense.

Chapter 8

What if my Cloud Provider goes out of business?:

As you depend on the Cloud and move your applications you will undoubtedly ask, "What if my Cloud Provider goes out of business? How do I get my data back?" With our Cloud offering we offer every client complete network documentation that clearly outlines how they could get it back in the event of an emergency. This includes information concerning our Network Security and Enterprise Privacy Liability insurance, information regarding your backups and licensing, detailed information of emergency contact numbers, and information on how to access your data and infrastructure without our assistance (although our plan is always to be there to support you). You should ask for this information from your Cloud provider.

We also upon request will give you a copy of OUR disaster recovery plan that shows what we've put in place to make sure we stay up and running. There are solutions available today that allow you to replicate your information between the Cloud and your local office or other Cloud provider such as Rack Space or Amazon Web Services. Doing this may give you the peace of mind you are looking for.

Chapter 9

New Hardware or Repurpose Existing?:

With any Cloud solution you will have multiple options with how to handle new, existing or current IT equipment. We often have clients asking, do I have to purchase new hardware (servers, workstations, thin clients) to move to the Cloud? The answer is No! That's one of the great benefits of Cloud Computing. It allows you to use older workstations, laptops and servers because the computing power is in the Cloud. Not only does this allow you to keep and use your IT hardware longer, but it allows you to buy lower end workstations and laptops because you don't need the expensive computing power required in the past. You can even repurpose older PC's and use them as a connecting device to access the cloud. With our Cloud solution, one available option is to have all PCs replaced with thin client machines at no cost to you. Additionally, we will replace any failed PC with a thin client so you don't have the unexpected capital expense of replacing the PC. We also provide a spare unit to remain onsite so there is minimal downtime if your PC or thin client should fail. Again, this is an example of how Cloud Computing can save you money and eliminates capital expenses.

Chapter 10

Is my Cloud Network PCI, HIPPA compliant?:

The quick answer is yes, compliancy is obtainable! Neither your Cloud solution nor your current IT solution is or was compliant straight out of the box. Compliancy is obtainable by having a third party company run a scan on your traditional or the Cloud network infrastructure to see what is not meeting the minimal requirements. These reports tell you what modifications need to take place in order for you to be compliant. We assist clients in assuring their information meets these standards.

Additionally e-mail can be archived and searchable. With each solution, you have different needs and requests. Having e-mail available, searchable and archived is a feature required for certain financial institutions compliances and is also obtainable.

Compliance can also be ensured in either environment by putting policies and procedures into place. Using a policy manager you can set passwords to require a certain number of letters and characters, set passwords to expire every x number of days, user groups for security purposes and ensuring the correct employees have access and the others don't. There are countless polices that can be enabled.

Chapter 11

Standardization and Interoperability:

Today's desktops are anything but standardized, companies run out and buy whatever is on the shelf at the office store or what's on special at an online retailer. Let's look at desktops and maintenance. Today, if you want to hire a new employee and need to purchase or replace desktops you have to order the new PC, buy the licensing for various software, user licensing for your servers, e-mail etc., wait two to five days for it to be delivered, get your IT vendor or IT department to un-box it, set it up, join it to the network, install applications and download updates. Then the tech needs to configure the user, user access and permissions, e-mail setup, e-mail filter setup, add user to appropriate groups, and ensure user has access to the correct printers, on and on and on. It's a big capital expense and takes a lot of time. If that new position doesn't work out, you still have the burden of a large outlay of capital for the labor, loss of time and you retain the equipment.

The Cloud model solves a lot of these headaches. Your Cloud provider should give you or an office manager access to a control panel and by following through a new user wizard, you can enter their first and last names; choose which applications they will use and what the e-mail address is for them. Connect either a thin client PC, laptop or desktop up to the network with a monitor, keyboard and mouse and within a few minutes that user will be able to send and receive company e-mails and access to your company's software applications. The best part is, your monthly Cloud usage will increase by one additional user with zero dollars in capital spent.

Cloud Desktops are easier to maintain than your traditional desktops. You can do security updates, software updates and modifications to one unit and apply the new standard to all users. This keeps you from having to go around to every desktop or laptop to install the updates separately and avoids the missed PCs due to them not being in the office. This is a huge time and money saver. Additionally, it reduces the need for an onsite IT person.

Chapter 12

Scalability:

Cloud Computing offers the ability like never before to grow or shrink your IT inventory with a click of the mouse. If it is business critical crunch time for your business and you need increased performance from your server, we can increase performance by adding additional processors, additional RAM or even storage capacity without a capital expense and without downtime. For example, a CPA firm may want to increase the speed of its servers during the peak of tax season and then cut back on resources during non-peak season. With traditional IT, you buy it and own it and have wasted resources sitting unused. When tax season is over, you simply reduce the resources back to what they were pre tax season.

If you are considering a new software application and want to test it because you're not sure it's a good fit for your company. We can setup a server in your environment and allow you to run your new application for one or two months before making the decision to move forward with it (provided the software vendor will allow you a trial period). If you decide to not use the program, we simply turn off the server. You will only be charged additionally for the time and resources of that server during testing. If you decide to use it, your monthly fee will increase by the amount of resources we activated for this applications usage.

Cloud Computing in this aspect is a great solution for startup companies that are not sure how much growth they will have. If they buy a low budget server and business starts booming, they will need to replace and disrupt their growing business by replacing the under resourced equipment.

Chapter 13

Technologies are NOT the Cloud:

Technologies such as Microsoft Terminal Services, Citrix XenApp Server, Citrix Receiver, virtual server and VMWare, etc. are technologies or software and can be used for Cloud Computing. These aforementioned are NOT by themselves Cloud Computing. Don't be fooled by a savvy IT person throwing around a lot of acronyms and technology terms. The following technologies are very useful in building and streamlining the foundation of the Cloud infrastructure.

Microsoft Terminal Services (aka RDP Remote Desktop Protocol) is Microsoft server software that allows a remote user to control a session on a Windows server. The experience is much like a Windows XP or Windows 7 desktop environment but all processing happens on the terminal server itself.

Citrix Xenapp Server is software that rides along with Windows Terminal Services and delivers the individual desktop and applications over the Internet as if they are running local. This is a nice addition to the Windows Terminal Services as it increases the speed delivery and reduces the total amount of data being sent and received across the remote connection.

Citrix Receiver is the application that is installable on multiplatform devices such as PCs tablets, Smartphone's, iPads, etc... This software can be downloaded from iTunes, Marketplace or via Citrix.com and allows you to connect securely from your device to your remote desktop environment hosted in the Cloud.

VMware software provides a virtualized set of hardware to run on the host operating system. The virtual environment allows you to use one physical server to run multiple server instances. An example of this is we have a client that has approximately 27 virtual servers on three physical hardware servers. This alone will lower IT cost for power, equipment, space, environment variables, etc. VMware software allows multiple servers to share hardware resources such as a video adapter, a network adapter and hard disk adapters. The host provides pass-through drivers for guest USB, serial, and parallel devices. Virtual machines running this way can be transferred to other servers running this software to allow easy in place upgrades with zero downtime for the user. A system can be paused on one virtual machine guest, move or copy that guest to another physical computer, and there resume execution exactly at the point of suspension. Alternatively, for enterprise servers, a feature called VMotion allows the migration of operational guest virtual machines between similar but separate hardware hosts sharing the same storage. Each of these transitions is completely transparent to any users on the virtual machine at the time it is being migrated.

Sorry to get so technical but I wanted you to understand that these are technologies used in delivering the Cloud but NOT Cloud Computing by themselves. Also these are just a few of the many technologies that are available in helping to deliver the applications across the Internet securely and at high availability. Also please remember this is not a technical manual and the list above is only a drop in the bucket.

Chapter 14

What to Look For When Hiring a Cloud Integrator:

A "Cloud Integrator" is a fancy name for an IT consultant who helps you set up and integrate the various software and solutions into a Cloud service specific for your business. But buyer beware! The Cloud is a new technology term but has been used for years. You don't want just anyone setting up your network on this type of a solution. You need to verify that they have been doing Cloud for a few years.

Unfortunately, the computer repair and consulting industry (along with many others) has its own share of incompetent or unethical people who will try to take advantage of trusting business owners who simply do not have the ability to determine whether or not they know what they are doing. Sometimes this is out of greed for your money; more often it's simply because they don't have the skills and competency to do the job right <u>but won't tell you that up front because they want to make the sale</u>.

From misleading information, unqualified technicians and poor management, to terrible customer service, we've seen it all and we know they exist in abundance because we have had a number of customers come to us for assistance in cleaning up the disaster they have caused.

Automotive repair shops, electricians, plumbers, lawyers, realtors, dentists, doctors, accountants, etc. are heavily regulated to protect the consumer from receiving substandard work or getting ripped off. However, the computer industry is still highly unregulated and there are few laws in existence to protect the consumer – **which is why it's so important for you to carefully research the company or person you are considering, to make sure they have the experience to set up, migrate and support your network to the Cloud.**

Anyone can promote themselves as a Cloud expert. Even if they are honestly *trying* to do a good job for you, their inexperience can cost you dearly in your network's speed and performance or in lost or corrupt data files. There are a lot of startup companies offering Cloud Solutions to small IT firms. These companies are ramping up quick but I am not sure they can sustain and I know I wouldn't put my client on a Cloud solution that was literally less than a year old. To that end, the next chapter has a number of questions you should ask your IT person before letting them migrate your network to the Cloud:

Chapter 15

Critical Questions To Ask Your IT Company Or Computer Consultant BEFORE Letting Them Move Your Network To The Cloud (Or Touch Your Network!)

Q1: How many clients have you provided Cloud services for to date and can you provide references?

Our Answer: You don't want someone practicing on your network. At a minimum, make sure they have done at least five implementations and are using the technology themselves.

Q2: How quickly do they guarantee to have a technician working on an outage or other problem?

Our Answer: Anyone you pay to support your network should provide upon request a written SLA (service level agreement) that outlines exactly how IT issues get resolved and in what time frame. I would also request that they reveal what their average resolution time has been with current clients over the last 12-36 months.

They should also answer their phones live from Mon – Fri 8:00 a.m. to 5:00 p.m. and provide you with an emergency after-hours number you may call if a problem should arise, including weekends.

If you cannot access your network because the Internet is down or due to some other problem, you can't be waiting around for hours for someone to call you back OR (more importantly) start working on resolving the issue. Make sure you get your IT vendors (SLA) Service Level Agreement in writing; often cheaper or less experienced consultants won't have this or will try and convince you it's not important or that they can't do this. Don't buy that excuse! They are in the business of providing IT support so they should have some guarantees or standards around this that they are willing to share with you.

Q3: What's your plan for transitioning our network to the Cloud to minimize problems and downtime?

Our Answer: Your Cloud Integrator should run a simultaneous Cloud environment during the transition and don't "turn off" the old network until everyone is 100% confident that everything has been transitioned and is working effortlessly. You don't want someone to switch your network overnight without setting up a test environment first. This will also allow you to keep a safety net in place to fall back on in the event of an unforeseen issue.

Q4: Do you provide a no risk trial of our network in the Cloud to test the proof of concept BEFORE we commit to a long-term contract?

Our Answer: Your Cloud Integrator should be able to provide a client with a 30 day Cloud "test drive" using your applications and data so you can see first hand what it will be like for you and your staff to move your servers to the Cloud. While this isn't a full migration, and will not be companywide trial, you should focus on the primary users testing this environment. This trial will give you a true feel for what Cloud Computing will be like BEFORE committing to a long-term contract. There is no charge for this and no obligation to buy anything. At the end of the 30 days, you'll know whether or not this is a right fit for you, or if you would prefer to keep your current onsite network.

Q5: Do they take the time to explain what they are doing and answer your questions in terms that you can understand (not geek speak), or do they come across arrogant and make you feel stupid for asking simple questions?

Our Answer: Our technicians are trained to have the 'heart of a teacher' and will take time to answer your questions and explain everything in simple terms and plain English.

Q6: How will your data be secured and backed up?

Our Answer: If they tell you that your data will be stored in their own co-location center in the back of their office, what happens if THEY get destroyed by a fire, flood or other disaster? What are they doing to secure the office and access? Are they backing it up somewhere else? What happens if they lose power? Make sure their data center is SAS 70 certified and they have a failover plan in place to ensure continuous service in the event that their location goes down. You will also want to find out how your data being backed up.

Q7: Do they have adequate errors and omissions insurance as well as workers' compensation insurance to protect YOU?

Our Answer: Here's something to consider: if THEY cause a problem with your network that causes you to be down for hours or days or to lose data, who's responsible? Here's another question to consider: if one of their technicians gets hurt at your office, who's paying? In this litigious society we live in, you better make sure that whomever you hire is adequately insured with both errors and omissions insurance AND worker's compensation and don't be shy about asking to see their latest insurance policies!

True Story: A few years ago a national "Geek" PC repair company was slapped with multi-million dollar lawsuits from customers for the bad behavior of their technicians. In some cases, their techs where accessing, copying and distributing personal information they gained access to on customer's PCs and laptops brought in for repairs. In other cases, they lost client's laptops (and subsequently all the data on them) and tried to cover it up. Bottom line: make sure the company you are hiring has proper insurance to protect YOU.

Q8: Is it standard procedure for them to provide you with written network documentation detailing what software licenses you own, your critical passwords, user information, hardware inventory, etc., or are they the only person with the "keys to the kingdom?"

Our Answer: All clients can receive this in written and electronic form at no additional cost. We also perform a quarterly update on this material and make sure certain key people from your organization have access to this information and know how to use it, giving you complete control over your network.

Side Note: You should NEVER allow an IT person to have that much control over you and your company. If you get the sneaky suspicion that your current IT person is keeping this under their control as a means of job security, get rid of them. This is downright unethical and dangerous to your organization, so don't tolerate it!

Q9: Do they have other technicians on staff that are familiar with your network in case your regular technician goes on vacation or gets sick?

Our Answer: Yes; and since we keep detailed network documentation (basically a blueprint of your computer network) and updates on every client's account, any of our technicians can pick up where another left off.

Q10: Do they INSIST on doing periodical test restores of your backups to make sure the data is not corrupt and could be restored in the event of a disaster?

Our Answer: We perform a monthly "fire drill" and perform a test restore from backup for our clients to make sure their data CAN be recovered in the event of an emergency. Upon completion and request we give our clients a report showing this test restore was conducted and that all systems are "OK". If there's a problem, we resolve it the same day. After all, the WORST time to "test" a backup is when you desperately need it.

Q11: Is their help-desk US-based or outsourced to an overseas company or third party?

Our Answer: We provide our own in-house helpdesk and make sure the engineers are friendly and helpful.

We consider this one of the most important aspects of customer service, plus we feel it's an important step in keeping your data secure.

Q12: Are they familiar with (and can they support) your unique line of business applications?

Our Answer: We own the problems with all line of business applications for our clients. That doesn't mean we can fix faulty software – but we WILL be the liaison between you and your vendor to resolve problems you are having and make sure these applications work smoothly for you instead of pointing fingers and putting you in the middle.

Q13: When something goes wrong with your Internet service, phone systems, printers or other IT services, do they own the problem or do they say "that's not our problem to fix?"

Our Answer: We feel WE should own the problem for our clients so they don't have to try and resolve any of these issues on their own – that's just plain old good service and something many computer guys won't do.

Q14: Can I keep a copy of my data replicated between the Cloud and my office?

Our Answer: Yes, if you would like to have all your files and folders replicated between the Cloud servers and the server(s) at your office, we can use

Distributed File System (DFS) to replicate the data. This will however increase your cost and requires a robust Internet connection, firewall device that is capable of connecting a VPN.

Chapter 16

What Our Clients Have To Say about Moving to the Cloud:

Nashville Computer has been hosting our server for over 4 years. Our initial need was two-fold: we had an extremely valuable employee whose husband was transferred across the country. Upgrading our server meant that we could keep a valuable resource that was already trained on our staff and still serve our clientele. Secondly, it allowed me, the business owner, to work from home on nights and weekends without having to leave family to go to the office. Cloud computing literally saved our business when Nashville experienced a major flood. On that memorable Sunday morning in May, I was out checking on the flood waters when I saw the maintenance crews at my office door. I waded in to open up my office door to be greeted by gushing water. I immediately phoned the emergency number for Nashville Computer to see what I needed to do. What a relief when they told me to go home because all my files were safe. My service has been down once in 4 years and it was due to an exterior problem that was out of their control. I can recommend Nashville Computer today because of this sole outage. Nashville Computer was prepared for the unexpected and had me back in business within 20 minutes. We rely heavily on the use of computers but we are not a technology firm. We need a technology partner so that we can concentrate on our business. Nashville Computer is our partner.

Edie Spain
Numbers Numbers LLC

"Our association with Nashville Computer spans many years. They have always provided us with superior customer service. The attention they give the customer is outstanding company wide. Their vast knowledge of the computer and IT business is paramount in the expertise they bring to the table. We are very fortunate to know and trust them with our needs." **Kay Brant**, *American Home Design*

"Nashville Computer understands the technology challenges of a small firm and has been prompt to respond to my service needs. With todays restricted technology budgets, and time constraints on Managerial staff, their knowledge and experience is a cost effective solution to IT Management." **Vickie Bates**, *Firm Administrator PLCS Law*

Glossary

Technical Terms Explained in Plain English:

ASP: *Application Service Provider*, a third-party company that manages and distributes software-based services and solutions to their customers over a wide-area network, usually the Internet.

Content Filtering: Software that prevents users from accessing or sending objectionable content via your network. Although this usually refers to Web content, many programs also screen inbound and outbound e-mails for offensive and confidential information. This software is not designed for virus, worm or hacker prevention.

CPU: *Central Processing Unit*, the brains of a computer.

Distributed File System (DFS): A Microsoft software feature that allows replication of files and folders between servers in a single or multiple locations. Used primarily in a Hybrid Cloud solution.

Firewall: A device or software program designed to protect your network from unauthorized access over the Internet. It may also provide Network

Address Translation (NAT) and Virtual Private Network (VPN) functionality.

Fractional T-1: Type of Internet connection obtained through an Internet Service Provider, used for both phone and Internet usage. T-1 Speed is 1.5Mbps. One or more channels of a T-1 service. A complete T-1 carrier contains 24 channels, each of which provides 64 Kbps. Most phone companies also sell fractional T-1 lines, which provide less bandwidth but are less expensive.

HIPPA: Health Insurance Privacy and Portability Act, a set of federal guidelines that protect coverage levels for employees and also sets forth regulations on how employees' private information is handled and protected.

HITECH: Subtitle D of the (HIPPA) Health Information Technology for Economic and Clinical Health Act (HITECH Act), enacted as part of the American Recovery and Reinvestment Act of 2009, addresses the privacy and security concerns associated with the electronic transmission of health information.

Hosted Applications (i.e. Hosted SharePoint or Hosted Exchange): A service whereby a provider makes a software (i.e. e-mail) and space available on a server so its clients can host their data or run an application on that server.

SAS 70 Type I: (Statement of Accounting Standards No. 70) is an audit designed to assess the sufficiency of the service companies controls as of a particular date. Type I looked at the companies controls to see if they we sufficient and properly designed.

SAS70 Type II: (Statement of Accounting Standards No. 70) is an audit designed to assess the sufficiency of the service companies controls as of a particular date. Type II actually tested the controls to see if they were effectively working as designed.

SSAE16: (Statement on Standards for Attestation Engagements No. 16) Reporting on Controls at a Service Organization is the next evolution in examining a service provider's controls and rendering an opinion for the provider's customers. Also referred to as Service Organization Controls (SOC) SSAE 16 includes a number of improvements in the examination of service providers which will benefit CIO's and customers of IT service companies who found the SAS70 Type II audit reports lacking.

Thin Client: A smaller version of a PC, but with less functionality, usually used to connect to another PC or Server to do the main processing.

URL: *Uniform Resource Locator,* the global address of documents, Websites and other resources on the Web. i.e. http://www.NashvilleComputer.com

VoIP: *Voice-Over-IP*, a category of hardware and software that allows you to use the Internet to make phone calls and send faxes. This technology is becoming very popular with businesses and home users alike because it greatly reduces telephone costs.

VPN: *Virtual Private Network,* a network constructed by using public wires (the Internet) to connect nodes (usually computers and servers). A VPN uses encryption and other security mechanisms to ensure that only authorized users can access the network and the data it holds. This allows businesses to connect to other servers and computers located in remote offices, from home, or while traveling.

A Final Word...

The reason I published this book was to fortify business owners and executives with the basic knowledge they need to make a great decision when choosing a Cloud Computing Integrator. I believe a qualified computer consultant can contribute to your business success just like a great marketing consultant, attorney, accountant or financial advisor can.

The technology industry is ever changing, and growing at such a rapid pace, that most business owners can't keep up with all the latest whiz-bang gadgets, alphabet soup acronyms, and choices available to them. Plus, many of the "latest and greatest" technological developments have a shelf life of six months before they become obsolete or completely out-of-date. Sorting through this rapidly-moving mess of information to formulate an intelligent plan for growing a business requires a professional who not only understands technology and how it works, but also understands how people and businesses need to work with technology for progress.

Unfortunately, the complexity of technology makes it easy for a business owner to fall victim to an incompetent or dishonest computer consultant. When this happens, it creates feelings of mistrust toward all technology consultants and vendors, which makes it difficult for those of us striving to deliver exceptional value and service to our clients.

Therefore, my purpose is to not only give you the information you need to find an honest, competent computer consultant, but in doing so, to raise the standards and quality of services for all consultants in my industry.

I certainly want your feedback on the ideas in this book. If you choose a Cloud Integrator as I've outlined and they work, please send me your story. If you've had a bad experience, I want to hear those horror stories as well. If you have additional tips and insights that we haven't considered, please share them with me. I might even use them in a future book!

Again, the more aware you are of what it takes to find and hire great consultants in every aspect of your business—not just technology—the stronger your business will become. I am truly passionate about building an organization that delivers uncommon service to my clients. I want to help business owners see the true competitive advantages technology can deliver to your business, and not just view it as an expensive necessity and source of problems.

Your contributions, thoughts and stories pertaining to my goal will help make it possible. Please write, call or e-mail me with your ideas.

Below you will find information on how to request a FREE Cloud Readiness Assessment. This is, of course, provided for free with no obligations and no expectations on our part. I want to be clear that this is NOT a bait and switch offer or a trick to get you to buy something. My reputation for running an honest and trustworthy business is something I hold very dear. I would never jeopardize that in any way. So why are we offering something like this for free?

Two reasons:

1. We are simply offering this service as a risk-free "get to know us" offer to people with whom we haven't had the pleasure of doing business. Again, our goal is to allow you to make an informed and confident decision; offering this service is one way we can help you evaluate our services.

2. This will allow us to determine if we even CAN help you. Obviously we can't help everyone and Cloud Computing might not be a good fit for your particular circumstances. Conducting this Assessment enables us to perform a small service for you and give you a way of determining whether or not we're the right company for you without risking your money.

Looking forward to your call or e-mail!

Charles Henson
Vice-President, Chief Innovation Officer
Nashville Computer, Inc.
615-377-0054
Charles@nashvillecomputer.com

www.NashvilleComputer.com

FREE Cloud Readiness Assessment

As a prospective customer, we would like to offer you a FREE Cloud Readiness Assessment and cost analysis. We do require that you be within an hour driving distance to be eligible for the "free" assessment. This does not mean that we cannot provide services for clients outside of this area. We currently have Cloud clients in 10 states.

This Assessment has three parts:

1. **Cost Analysis and Inventory:** Our first step is to look at what your current network consists of in hardware, licenses, data, and applications. Next, we compile an IT cost assessment to reveal your total amount you spend on IT, including Internet connectivity, support and other fees. Most business owners have never really looked at their entire IT costs this way and often this report alone is an eye-opener. Why do we do this? Because our goal is to find ways we can significantly lower those costs while simplifying and improving your workflow.

2. **Health Check:** We will perform a *27 point assessment* of your entire network to look for potential problems, security loopholes, spyware and other hidden problems that you might not know about. Often we find faulty

backups, out-of-date anti-virus software, faulty firewalls and missing security patches that, if left un-addressed could end up costing you MORE in new hardware, support, and business downtime as well as data loss.

3. **Cloud Readiness:** After we've looked at the above areas, we then look at how you and your employees work and share information and see what applications or processes we can safely move to the Cloud to improve ease of use and, of course, lower costs.

When complete, we'll give you a Cloud Action Plan that shows you how we can save you money and resolve a number of work-around and solutions to problems you may have been experiencing to date. Even if you decide not to hire us, having a third party conduct this type of assessment will give you some good information on saving money and the security and health of your computer network.

Request Your FREE Cloud Readiness Assessment today:

http://www.nashvillecomputer.com/appointment/

About The Author

Charles Henson has been in the IT industry for over 20 years. He got his first "computer" around 1984 from a school friend. His thought was that if computers break, someone will need to fix them. This drove Charles to attend school and receive an Associates degree in Electrical Engineering from ITT Technical Institute. Charles is constantly looking for, reading about and learning new technologies as they become available. He feels that he needs to be the advisor to his clients. In May 2010 he was invited to the Google Headquarters in California for his personal feedback and opinions on the Google Adwords product offering and to give feedback on training that he took part in. Charles has been interviewed and featured in the Redman IT magazine regarding Backup Disaster Recovery solutions. He has worked with and has been trained on PKI (Public Key Infrastructure) a technology used to encrypt data and communications. Additionally he has been asked for his insight and invited to discussion groups and interviewed by peers and industry leaders to help build a common Cloud Computing Blueprint. Charles has been employed with Nashville Computer, Inc. since 1991 and currently serves as Vice-President and Chief Innovation Officer. Charles was born in Missouri and moved to Parsons TN when he was in middle school. He was in the Army National Guard for 8 years and served as a tank driver, mortar gunner, a marksman and trained at Fort Benning and Fort Campbell. He currently lives in Brentwood TN with his wife of more than 20 years and their two children. Charles often tells his potential clients "I am local and you may run into me in the store, in the park or while out with the family".

Nashville Computer, Inc. is a locally owned IT company specializing in Peace of Mind IT Solutions. Nashville Computer was started in 1988 as a software company providing organizations with MAS90 accounting applications. The need for computers to run the new software became increasingly important and so began selling hardware. With the need for businesses to share data and connectivity to the Internet, they grew from a hardware/software provider to a break-fix business and worked with clients to design, build, implement and maintain their network environments. For over 10 years, Nashville Computer has helped their client's setup remote locations and stay connected securely. Nashville Computer has been doing "Cloud Computing" as it is known today for over 10 years. Today Nashville Computer has 15 employees and oversees the monitoring and maintenance of over 200 servers and their daily backups and availability.

Technology Strategist and Cloud Expert for Small to Medium Business:

Charles Henson

Coauthor of

Hassle-Free Computer Support

Book Order Information

If you enjoyed this book, share it with others! Use this form to order extra copies for friends, colleagues, clients or members of your association. Please allow 2-4 weeks for delivery.

Quantity Discounts:

1-9 copies = $19.95 each, 10-49 copies = $16.95 each

50-99 copies = $13.95 each

100 or more copies = Call for discounts and wholesale prices

Book Order Form

Information:

Name: _____

Company: _____

Address: _____

City: _____

State/Province: _____

ZIP/Postal Code: _____

# of copies _____ @ $_____ Total: $_____

Add shipping and handling @ $3 per book: $_____

Please make check or money order payable to:

Nashville Computer

Credit Card: ☐Visa ☐MC ☐Amex ☐Discover

Card Number: _____

Expiration Date: _____

Signature: _____

Thank you for your order!

www.ingramcontent.com/pod-product-compliance
Lightning Source LLC
Chambersburg PA
CBHW061033050326
40689CB00012B/2797